Phyllis Schlafly Speaks, Volume 3

How the Republican Party Became Pro-Life

Phyllis Schlafly

Edited by Ed Martin

Permission to quote in critical reviews with citation:
How the Republican Party Became Pro-Life
By Phyllis Schlafly

ISBN 978-0-9984000-8-2

Skellig
AMERICA

TABLE OF CONTENTS

This book is dedicated to Kathleen Sullivan: in recognition of her fight for life and of her love for her friends.

There is nothing on this earth more to be prized than true friendship. ~ St. Thomas Aquinas

* * *

Of Kathleen Sullivan, Phyllis Schlafly would say with a wave of her hand: "Do whatever she says." Such trust by Phyllis was uncommon. Her trust in Kathleen was the fruit of over five decades of hard work and friendship.

In the Spring of 2016, Kathleen Sullivan arrived in St. Louis for what was scheduled as a short visit. She stayed for almost four months helping Phyllis through her final successes: in Cleveland, for Trump, and in death. Kathleen was, without exaggeration, a special blessing from the Lord to Phyllis and all of us.

Editor's Note by Ed Martin

A few years ago, a friend called. He had recently heard Phyllis Schlafly deliver a speech and was excited about it. The speech, entitled *"How the Republican Party became Pro-Life,"* had been delivered at his church pro-life committee and some of the members were asking if there was a transcript for them to pass on to friends.

I asked Phyllis about the pro-life speech. It was a speech she gave frequently over the years, she told me, and was her account of the fight to put the pro-life plank in the Republican Party platform. She was sure there was a copy of the speech around but she had delivered that speech recently without notes or text.

I turned to the archives in the Phyllis Schlafly Center here in Clayton, Missouri. With the help of our archives, Deb Pentecost, I found the text of this speech from 2004 in Dallas, Texas. When I read the speech, I realized it was a singularly great speech: filled with history, humor and insight. It was classic Phyllis!

i

I also thought the topic—the pro-life Republican Party—deserved great attention especially as we headed into 2016 and another Republican Convention and likely platform fight. I encouraged Phyllis to expand the speech into a book and over the ensuing year she did just that. You are holding the fruit of her labor.

When she finished writing this book, Phyllis told me she had a new perspective on the importance of her pro-life success. And, while she still celebrated her many other victories, I noticed her telling people about the lesson of the pro-life Republican platform plank fight: what was once deemed impossible became possible with hard work and smarts.

"It really made a difference" she said "and the Republican Party is the only pro-life party left."

She was right. It really made a difference and saved many babies. Thank the Good Lord and Phyllis Schlafly too.

* * *

Much of this book was originally published in Spring 2016 as a book entitled "How the Republican Party Became Pro-Life." It was timed to give Republicans a vision of how to keep the Republican Platform pro-life at the Republican National Convention in Cleveland in July 2016.

By the generosity of a pro-life supporter, over 10,000 copies of that earlier book were distributed to Republican delegates and others in Cleveland. It was among the gifts presented to attendees at the 2016 **Life of the Party** celebration, which Phyllis hosted at the Cleveland Browns football stadium with keynote speaker and dear friend of Phyllis, Coach Lou Holtz.

I have updated this volume to include the events of 2016 as they relate to the pro-life fight. I have also included the relevant parts of 2016 Republican Platform in this volume as an appendix. Phyllis called the 2016 platform the "most conservative platform ever" and credited Donald Trump with honoring his promise to Phyllis to "protect the platform."

* * *

This volume is the third in a series called Phyllis Schlafly Speaks. Each volume is organized around Phyllis' writings and speaking. Phyllis Schlafly's output as speaker and writer was so vast that it will take us decades to reprint what took her over seven decades in public life to create. We hope you will collect each volume in what will be many volumes: her wisdom, wit and insight on nearly every subject of historical significance makes it a wonderful challenge for an editor.

Foreword by Bob Novak

T he first I ever heard of Phyllis Schlafly was in 1964 when she published *A Choice Not an Echo*. She was a housewife from Alton, Illinois, forty years old, and I was a budding columnist. The late Roland Evans and I had just started our column in 1963. In 1964, I was a 33-year-old syndicated columnist. I read the book and I thought it was one of the best-written, most interesting, fascinating pieces of political advocacy that I had ever read in my life. And I wouldn't say I disagreed with everything in it, but damn near everything.

Now, I am in the process of writing my memoirs and I came across a copy of the book in the process and I sat down and read it all the way through ... I couldn't stop. And you know, forty years later, I agree with almost everything in it.

I tell people that I have had a long journey to the right and I say I get a little more Conservative every day. And they say, well there's no more room on the right for you to go.

(Pointing at Phyllis): Well, yes there is! I agree with Phyllis on almost everything now, but not everything. I'm working at it. And I hope I'll get there. She had been very important in guiding me to the right, which has been incremental and not sudden.

She's also been important in guiding somebody to the right who she may have met but she doesn't really know, and that's my wife. My wife, Geraldine, would die if she knew I was going to mention her name. She is one of the most private people I've ever met. When I met this Texas girl, she had never met a Republican until she was a grown woman. When I first met her in 1960, she was one of Sen. Lyndon Johnson's secretaries, a registered Democrat, and when I married her in 1962, she was Vice President Johnson's secretary. She has, in the course of time, changed her registration from Democrat to Republican. She has spent the last many years as a behind-the-scenes, fervent, pro-life activist. And she has been guided, although Phyllis didn't know it, by Phyllis Schlafly, all those years.

So, I thank Phyllis, and I also thank God for what has been a wonderful journey over these forty years. Because I say, it's been a great life for me, covering politics, making politicians uncomfortable, saying whatever I want to say, writing whatever I want to write. What a great country and what a great privilege that has been for me.

One of my favorite things over the years has been covering Republican platform hearings ... and watching Phyllis Schlafly in action at these hearings. It is awesome! Here is a person who holds no public office, usually not a party position, doesn't run a big lobbying firm, doesn't represent a big corporation or a special interest group, and she instills awe, fear, respect, and she has influence. I really do believe, that as Faith Whittlesey said, that the Republican Party, remaining a pro-life party, would not have been possible all these years if it had not been for the work at these platform hearings and sessions of Phyllis Schlafly. Because, presidential candidates, and even incumbent presidents (we won't name names) wanted to bail out on that issue, on many occasions, I can guarantee you.

At the last hearing, the last session of the platform committee at the Jacob Javits building in New York ... she was really awesome. People in the White House pulled for most of the members of the platform committee - even governors and wives... some little aide at the White House would say something and they would just collapse. But Phyllis has principles. And she, I believe, has not only influenced the draft of the platform, but she influenced how the changes were made. Did she win everything? Absolutely not. But she, believe me, was the only force from the outside that had any influence because all the platform committee members wanted to do was get along with the White House.

I would suppose everybody in this room, or nearly everybody, is for George W. Bush's re-election. I would certainly hope so. But I believe it is part of the Conservative movement and part of being an American that you don't salam when the people in power say you have to do something and Phyllis Schlafly has led the way on that.

Statement made by Bob Novak at Phyllis
Schlafly's 80th Birthday on September 18, 2004

First Skirmishes

Abortion law had traditionally been in the domain of the states, as was nearly all criminal law. Beginning in 1967, more than a dozen states weakened in various ways their laws that made abortion a crime. This movement was made easier because, in the 1960s, conventional wisdom told Americans that the earth was running out of food and we would face mass starvation when the earth could no longer feed our growing population. The implication was that people would be doing a good thing if they limited births.

This fallacy was promoted by the two-million-copy sale of the 1968 book called *The Population Bomb* by college professor Paul R. Ehrlich. I remember attending a dinner party hosted by a prominent neighbor who solemnly warned us that this might be our last roast beef dinner because America would soon be unable to afford to raise cattle for food.

Conventional concern about a worldwide problem of overpopulation and our duty to "do something" to save ourselves from a terrible fate reached the White House during the presidency of Richard Nixon. The United States Agency for International Development (USAID) began to spend millions on the "problem" of overpopulation.

On December 26, 1970, Nixon signed the Family Planning Services and Population Research Act (better known as Title X) creating a national commitment to provide adequate family planning services to all Americans who wanted them but couldn't afford them. This legislation on family planning and population had strong bipartisan support.

When Nixon sent this legislation to Congress, in 1969, he warned about the increasing rate of population growth and predicted that by the year 2000 the Earth would have eight billion people. To implement a national commitment to limit our population, Nixon asked for expanded research in contraceptive development. The National Center for Family Planning Services was established in what was then called the Department of Health, Education and Welfare.

The pro-abortion momentum was stalled by a defeat in the Illinois Legislature in 1969. However, in 1970, Planned Parenthood of New York City started the battle to legalize abortion in New York State. The tide of public opinion turned against abortion in 1971. Pro-abortion bills failed to pass in any state in 1971 and 1972. The New York legislature even repealed its two-year-old abortion-on-demand law (only to have the repeal vetoed by Governor Nelson Rockefeller). In November 1972, pro-abortion referenda were defeated by the voters in North Dakota with a 77 percent vote and in Michigan by a 61 percent vote.

Then, on January 22, 1973, the U.S. Supreme Court, in the preeminent act of judicial supremacy, struck down the anti-abortion laws of all states. As Justice Byron White wrote in dissent, *Roe v. Wade* was "an exercise of raw judicial power ... I find nothing in the language or history of the Constitution to support the Court's judgment." The only Republican justice who dissented was William Rehnquist.

A recent book called *Abuse of Discretion* by Clarke Forsythe spells out the judicial history of *Roe v. Wade*, describing its dishonesty and failure to follow proper judicial procedure and the Court's own precedents. Forsythe's book is based on a close review of the papers of eight of the nine justices who voted in *Roe v. Wade* or *Doe v. Bolton*. The justices originally agreed to hear those two cases only to decide the question of federal versus state jurisdiction.

But a Court crisis erupted in 1971 when two justices, Hugo Black and John Harlan, abruptly retired due to ill health. Reducing the number of justices to seven empowered a temporary majority of four Justices to use those two cases to sweep away all state abortion laws and declare a right to abortion.

Those two cases had no evidentiary record about abortion. There was no trial, no evidence, no expert witness, no record of expert testimony, and no medical data about abortion, its risks or its consequences. None of the statements of sociology, medicine or history used in the *Roe* decision were derived from evidence subjected to the adversary process.

The majority seized upon the claim in a Planned Parenthood brief that a first-trimester abortion is safer than childbirth. That unproved statement significantly influenced the justices to prohibit health and safety regulations in the first trimester, and to add a "health" exception after viability for any reason related to the woman's emotional "well-being."

During the next four decades, hard-fought battles about abortion were waged in Congress, state legislatures, and candidates' campaigns for public office. Various federal and state laws have made obtaining an abortion more difficult than at any time since the 1970s. Pro-life activists successfully lobbied for regulations that limit access, require waiting periods, require ultrasounds, impose safety regulations on clinics, and require minors to get a parent's permission. Fewer doctors are willing to perform abortions, and fewer abortion clinics are open for business.

Gallup polls report that support for abortion rights is fading, particularly among young Americans. More people now identify themselves as pro-life than pro-choice.

In 2014, a federal court upheld a Texas law that prohibits abortion unless the abortionist has hospital privileges within thirty miles. The purpose is so the abortionist can remain available to handle medical complications, instead of letting emergency room costs fall on the taxpayers. Nineteen abortion clinics immediately closed in Texas because of this law. This is the most effective law that states can pass to reduce abortions, and it has been imitated in other states.

The feminists consider abortion the fundamental, irreducible first commandment of feminism. It is usually shrouded in words such as choice, or reproductive freedom, or privacy, or even equal rights, but to feminists, abortion is much more than that. It is the keystone of feminist power over men. As Gloria Steinem opined, the "right of reproductive freedom … attacks the very foundation of patriarchy."

Supreme Court justices Kennedy, O'Connor, and Souter, in *Planned Parenthood v. Casey*, explained the centrality of abortion to feminist ideology. They wrote that, "the ability of women to participate equally in the economic and social life of the Nation has been facilitated by their ability to control their reproductive lives."

The abortion dogma has always had a strong anti-male element. Feminists persuaded the Supreme Court to rule not only that the father has no say as to whether his own baby is killed, but even that the woman has a right *not* to tell her husband that his baby is being killed.

Abortion is the litmus test of whether or not you are feminist. Feminists have even made support of abortion the test of whether a political candidate is waging a "war on women."

When the Supreme Court legalized abortion in *Roe v. Wade* in 1973, many people said the Supreme Court has spoken and *that* ends the debate. But *Roe v. Wade* did not end the controversy; it was the beginning of a long legal and political battle. The American people are not willing for unelected judges to rule our nation.

1976

Starting Republicans on a New Road

G erald Ford became President in August 1974. He was the only person who ever became President without ever having been nominated for President or Vice President by a Party's National Convention or elected President or Vice President by the voters. Ford was a beneficiary of the 25th Amendment to the U.S. Constitution ratified in 1967. President Nixon was forced to resign after Vice President Spiro Agnew resigned, so the 25th Amendment elevated the unelected Vice President Gerald Ford to the office of President.

First Lady Betty Ford wasted no time in lining up with the feminist movement, declaring *Roe v. Wade* a "great, great decision." When she appeared on CBS 60 Minutes in August 1975, she announced her support of legalized abortion, suggested that premarital sex might cut down on the divorce rate, and said she would not criticize her daughter if she entered into an extramarital affair. Most Republicans pretended not to notice her extremist remarks.

Betty Ford was in line with Republican Party officialdom. Republican National Committee Chair Mary Louise Smith supported abortion rights, and New York Governor Nelson Rockefeller took a leading role in the fight for abortion rights in New York.

The first Republican National Convention after *Roe v. Wade* was in 1976 in Kansas City, Missouri. That year, I served on a subcommittee of the Platform Committee. I offered a motion to include a plank to "protest the Supreme Court's intrusion into the family structure" and to pledge "to seek enactment of a constitutional amendment to restore protection of the right to life for unborn children." The subcommittee approved that language by a vote of thirteen to one, and it was easily approved by the full Platform Committee and then by the National Convention.

At this National Convention, most conservatives were hoping to nominate Ronald Reagan on this, his second try for the nomination. However, the 1976 Convention nominated

Gerald Ford over Ronald Reagan by the narrow vote of 1,187 to 1,070.

U.S. Senator Jesse Helms decided that the 1976 Platform was the place to stand and fight for conservative principles that had eroded under President Gerald Ford, who took advice on most important decisions from Henry Kissinger. It was a tremendous victory for conservatives when the 1976 Convention adopted Jesse Helms' Platform, which repudiated the Nixon-Ford-Kissinger policies about nuclear testing and about accommodation and detente with the Soviet Union.

It was also significant that the 1976 Republican Convention was the first national Convention when the emerging pro-family movement raised its voice in national politics, daring to challenge the U.S. Supreme Court on *Roe v. Wade*.

At the very end of the Convention, President Ford spontaneously turned the microphone over to Reagan, who then delivered one of the most dramatic speeches in all convention history. Speaking extemporaneously for less than five minutes, Reagan reminded his delegates of their accomplishment. "Our Platform is a banner of bold unmistakable colors with no pastel shades," he said. One of those bold unmistakable colors was the first adoption of a Republican Party pledge to "restore protection of the right to life for unborn children."

Some people were hoping that the Democratic Party would also take an anti-abortion position, and a pro-life Democrat, Ellen McCormack of New York, ran for the Democratic nomination for President. She was on the ballot in 18 states and raised enough money to qualify for federal matching funds and Secret Service protection. Her name was placed in nomination at the 1976 Democratic National Convention, but she received only 22 votes. After Mrs. McCormack's valiant effort, the Democratic Party became increasingly inhospitable to pro-life candidates.

1980

Pro-Life Republicans Make Waves

A t the 1980 Republican National Convention in Detroit, Michigan, conservative Republicans expected to nominate Ronald Reagan, who had failed to win the nomination so narrowly four years earlier. By the time the Convention convened, it had become clear that (despite the opposition of the kingmakers) Reagan had enough Delegates to be nominated for President. So the media decided to make the big Convention news my fight to remove support of the Equal Rights Amendment (ERA) from the Republican Platform, where it had been resting without controversy for decades.

We didn't realize it until years later, but a major reason why the feminists were so eager to get the Republican Party platform to eliminate support for ERA was that the feminists believed (and later argued in court) that, if ERA put "sex" in the U.S. Constitution, that would force the government to use federal and state taxpayer funds to pay for abortions.

Endorsement of ERA had been a line in the Republican Platform since 1940, and nobody paid much attention to it. However, when the feminists made it a big issue in 1980 and lined up VIPs such as Helen Milliken, wife of the Governor of Michigan; Margaret Heckler, U.S. Congresswoman from Massachusetts; and Mary Dent Crisp, the Republican Party co-chairman, to picket in the streets in favor of ERA, it became necessary for those against ERA to engage in the fight.

We wanted ERA out of the Platform especially because, since Reagan publicly opposed ERA, Platform endorsement of ERA would be an embarrassment to him. The media made the ERA issue a huge media controversy. Later on, when I reviewed the ten years of network TV coverage of the Equal Rights Amendment, 1972 to 1982, I found that 50 percent of the television network minutes devoted to ERA pertained to the 1980 Republican Convention in Detroit.

The media were shocked when the Human Resources Subcommittee, chaired by then-Representative Trent Lott of Mississippi, voted eleven to four for a Women's Rights section that excluded ERA. The media went into cardiac arrest when the full Platform Committee approved the subcommittee's action by a vote of ninety to nine. The media set up a debate between me and Michigan Governor William Milliken on the Today Show, but when the day came, Milliken chickened out and sent Congresswoman Margaret Heckler in his place.

At every Republican Convention, members of the Platform Committee were entertained with a beautiful buffet supper on Sunday evening before the meetings started on Monday. I was not on the Platform Committee in 1980, so I wasn't invited, but I arranged to attend the party on Senator Jesse Helms' arm, so nobody stopped me. Some of our best Eagle advocates were also able to attend the supper party: Najla Lataif, Tottie Ellis, and Shirley Curry. They lobbied the Platform Committee very effectively! The 1980 Platform reaffirmed "support of a constitutional amendment to restore protection of the right to life for unborn children," and added, "We also support the Congressional efforts to restrict the use of taxpayers' dollars for abortion." The feminists' effort to weaken this anti-abortion language failed in the Platform Committee, seventy-five to eighteen.

14

Of course, all Republican National Convention procedures, including voting on the Platform and on all its sections (especially controversial ones), had to go through the relevant subcommittee, and then the full Platform Committee, and finally win approval by the full Convention of some two thousand Delegates. Nearly every change in the Platform had to run the gauntlet of articulate speakers who expressed passionate opinions.

After the subcommittee spent a long afternoon debating and finally agreeing on the language of the section of the Platform about abortion, I realized we would soon be adjourning for dinner, and there would be an unplanned evening when the powers-that-be could attempt to badger, threaten, persuade, or intimidate some subcommittee members (who often were new to the political process) to change their votes. About 6:00 p.m., facing many hours between then and the scheduled meeting of the full Platform Committee at 9:00 a.m. the next morning, I rushed out into the hall and ran into Jimmy Lyons, a wealthy Republican from Houston. I said, "Jimmy, don't you belong to some club in Houston with privileges here in Detroit where we can take this important Subcommittee to dinner?" He replied, "I don't know, but I'll

15

find out."

Jimmy disappeared into a phone booth (this was the pre-cell-phone era when we used phone booths). About ten minutes later, Jimmy came back and said, "I've got you all set up at the Detroit Athletic Club." Of course the dozen members of the subcommittee accepted this gracious invitation, and the party didn't break up until nearly midnight. Several members of the Subcommittee were articulate advocates of our pro-life mission and the flaky members lacked the nerve and the facts to challenge them.

I learned later that the chairman of the Platform Committee, U.S. Senator John Tower of Texas, who was not pro-life, had spent the entire evening trying to call all our Subcommittee members but couldn't reach a single one.

The full Platform Committee convened on schedule at 9:00 a.m. the next morning and approved all our Subcommittee's language.

After those votes were recorded, the co-chairman of the Republican Party, Mary Dent Crisp, who opposed the pro-life

16

plank, went out to meet the press and shed real tears before the television cameras. She then left the Republican Party to support John Anderson as a Third Party candidate, trying to defeat Ronald Reagan. Anderson received only seven percent of the popular vote.

The pro-abortion feminists suffered such a shellacking in Detroit about ERA, they didn't have any energy left to fight the pro-lifers for the votes of the full Convention. We had no difficulty in keeping our pro-life plank in the Platform.

Reagan's election as President in 1980 profoundly changed politics in America. Reagan ended the Nixon-Ford-Kissinger era of detente. Reagan mainstreamed conservatism based on middle-American fiscal and family values. Reagan's vision of conservatism consisted of four elements: limited government with lower taxes; personal responsibility that rejects taxpayer handouts; military superiority to protect American independence; and respect for life and family values.

Each of those four elements has a large constituency and attracted many pro-family Democrats and independents to vote Republican. Reagan gave Americans a true choice, not an

17

echo of all the previous presidential campaigns. In his First Inaugural Address, Reagan proclaimed, "Government is not the solution to our problem; government is the problem."

1984

Locking Pro-Life Into the Platform

T he Republican National Convention in 1984 in Dallas was the most successful and enjoyable of all Republican Conventions in the 20th century.

Members of the National Republican Platform Committee are elected by the members of each state's delegation, and the elections are gender specific. One man and one woman are elected to the Platform Committee from each state.

Congressman Henry Hyde and I were the two Delegates elected to the Platform Committee from Illinois, and we led the Committee in adopting this strong and beautiful language:

"The unborn child has a fundamental, individual right to life which cannot be infringed. We therefore reaffirm our support for a human life amendment to the Constitution, and

19

we endorse legislation to make clear that the Fourteenth
Amendment's protections apply to unborn children. We
oppose the use of public revenues for abortion and will
eliminate funding for organizations which advocate or support
abortion. … We reaffirm our support for the appointment of
judges at all levels of the judiciary who respect traditional
family values and the sanctity of innocent human life."

.•

Representative Trent Lott was the chairman of the 1984
national Platform Committee. The pro-life plank wasn't
particularly controversial except for a couple of tantrums
staged for the media by Senator Lowell Weicker and
Representative Nancy Johnson, both from Connecticut. On a
voice vote, the full Convention adopted the Platform including
our strong pro-life section.

Eagle Forum members have sponsored a party at every
Republican National Convention starting in 1964. Our event
during the 1984 Convention was a memorable fashion show.
Every prominent Republican lady walked in that fashion show,
led by Mrs. Jesse Helms and Mrs. Jack Kemp.

Ronald Reagan won reelection in November 1984. He

and the Platform offered voters a clear-cut choice on the issues that matter to Americans: pro-life; national defense; military superiority; fiscal limitation; and pro-family policies.

Instead of Kissinger-style pessimism and defeatism, Reagan offered "morning in America." The 27 million conservatives who voted for Barry Goldwater in 1964 increased their numbers to 54 million in 1984.

1988

Let the Good Times Roll

T he 1988 Republican National Convention was scheduled to take place in New Orleans, and Republicans were ready to "let the good times roll." A few Delegates toyed with nominating Jack Kemp or Phil Gramm for President, but George H.W. Bush had flawlessly played the role of second fiddle to Ronald Reagan for eight years (as though he had been singing George Gershwin's "Bidin' My Time") so Bush was easily nominated.

The Family and Community Subcommittee approved the Platform with the same pro-life language that was in the 1984 Platform by a vote of eleven to three, and the full Convention adopted the Platform by a unanimous voice vote.

The Reagan coalition of fiscal and social conservatives loyally stuck together. With Peggy Noonan writing his speeches, George H.W. Bush sounded like Ronald Reagan and voters assumed Bush would continue Reagan's agenda. Indeed, voters almost looked upon Bush's election in 1988 as voting for Ronald Reagan's "third term."

George Bush had the good fortune to draw Massachusetts' Michael Dukakis as his opponent. While most politicians were trying to avoid the label of liberal, Dukakis proudly announced himself "a liberal Democrat" and "a card-carrying member" of the American Civil Liberties Union. Dukakis gave us liberalism in one package – a synthesis of Walter Mondale on taxes, Ted Kennedy and Tip O'Neill on spending, Geraldine Ferraro on abortion, and George McGovern on foreign policy.

Bush offered the voters a choice, not an echo on patriotic, economic, social and pro-life issues, and voters found it easy to make him the 1988 winner. We successfully kept the Republican pro-life commitment in the Party's Platform with the strong 1984 language.

After George H.W. Bush became President, however, he abandoned many policies of his patron, Ronald Reagan, and returned to the big-government and globalist policies of his wealthy friends. Almost the only conservative thing Bush did while President was his nomination of Clarence Thomas to the U.S. Supreme Court. That was, indeed, a great thing for America. Thomas has served as an outstanding constitutionalist and pro-life Justice.

1992

The Year of the Red Cowboy Hats

T rouble started for pro-lifers in 1990. The pro-abortionists began a major campaign to try to scratch pro-life out of the Republican Party and its Platform. A GOP fundraiser, Ann Stone, announced that she had reinvigorated a Planned Parenthood group called "Republicans for Choice" and intended to raise three million dollars to take the pro-life plank out of the Republican Platform.

Almost simultaneously, Mary Dent Crisp, who had been absent politically since her announced support of third-party candidate John Anderson in 1980, started another organization with the same goal. That was very heavy artillery because, of course, they had the media on their side plus many big donors. Conventional wisdom predicted that, at the next Convention in 1992 in Houston, the pro-life plank would become history.

With easy access to the media, Crisp and Stone launched well-publicized threats to remove the pro-life plank from the Republican Platform. They played their trump card in announcing that First Lady Barbara Bush wanted the pro-life plank deleted. However, members of the Platform Committee had worked hard to be elected, so they had minds of their own and remained staunchly pro-life.

The Platform Committee scheduled a special public hearing in Salt Lake City for May 16. When Delegates arrived in Salt Lake City, they were greeted with many billboards and signs reading "Pro Choice." Nicholas Graham, the spokesman for the National Republican Coalition for Choice, announced, "We are going to be a very loud, very annoying voice from here straight through to Houston." The *New York Times* reported that the pro-abortion faction appeared "willing to cause political discomfort for President Bush by waging a public campaign."

At the time that pro-abortion groups made their provocative announcements, three of our best Eagle Forum leaders happened to be in Chicago attending a meeting: Colleen Parro, who was our key Eagle working with me and

General Daniel Graham of High Frontier to support President Reagan in the building of a strong U.S. anti-missile defense; Kathleen Sullivan, president of Illinois Eagle Forum; and Penny Pullen, an Illinois State Representative who was the pro-life leader in the Illinois Legislature.

When they heard the news about the new pro-abortion campaign, they immediately went to a phone booth, called me and said, "We have to do something!" "Well," I replied, "America has many good pro-life organizations. They can take care of this problem."

I then phoned all the national pro-life organizations and asked them if they were going to take on the project of stopping those prominent women, who had the support of money and the media, from taking the pro-life plank out of the Republican Platform. They all said "No" because they wanted to be non-partisan and not ally their organizations with any political party.

Well, I've never been nonpartisan. I believe the Republican Party must be the vehicle to achieve the good things we want for our country, which is why I've run for and been elected a Republican Convention Delegate so many times. The bottom line was, "Phyllis, you have to do it." So Colleen Parro and I started Republican National Coalition for Life.

To launch our new organization, I planned a special luncheon at a top-scale hotel in Washington, DC with several people we wanted to join our effort – Beverly LaHaye, Gary Bauer, and a couple of major donors I was hoping would help finance our new project. I alerted the hotel that one of those important donors, Pat Rooney, was a vegetarian, so he should be given a nice vegetarian plate. In the middle of my impassioned speech asking for support for our new organization, the waiter walked in with a big plate that had nothing on it except twelve sprigs of broccoli arranged like a clock and a lonely carrot in the middle. That threw my speech off course, but we survived the interruption and continued to spell out our goals.

It wasn't hard to anticipate that we would face a big fight about abortion at the Republican National Convention in Houston in 1992 when George H.W. Bush would be up for re-nomination. He was declining in the polls and squishing on pro-life, and the pro-abortion crowd thought they had a good opportunity to change course for Republicans.

Colleen Parro did a fantastic job of identifying pro-life and Eagle Forum leaders in a majority of states, urging them to become Delegates to their state Republican Convention. She educated them on how to run for and get elected as Delegates A to the Republican National Convention and how to run for and win a seat on the national Platform Committee. RNC for Life B booths cropped up at state conventions across the country, equipped with red, white and blue banners, bumper stickers, and RNC/Life buttons. By the time we arrived at the 1992 Convention, we had identified our pro-life Delegates and believed that, if a floor fight occurred, we would win.

It's not easy to be elected a Delegate to a Republican Convention. I had to be elected at a caucus of my Township, 1 and then elected again in a caucus of my State Legislative 2 District, and then elected again in my Congressional District 3 caucus and elected again by the state Republican convention. 4 Then, to be on the Platform Committee I had to be elected by a vote at the first caucus of all the state's elected national 5 Convention Delegates. This takes planning and making friends with people active in the Republican Party. (We now need

29

hundreds of pro-lifers to make similar plans to be elected to the 2016 Convention, which is scheduled to be in Cleveland, Ohio.)

In 1992, we set a goal to get all Republican public officials to sign a pledge to support the pro-life plank in the Platform, and we did get nearly all the prominent Republicans to sign our pledge, from Newt Gingrich on down to local officeholders. We packaged the tens of thousands of signed pledges in a separate decorated and labeled box for each of the fifty states.

To make a splash at the Republican Convention in Houston, we decided that our insignia would be red cowboy hats. We bought three thousand large red cowboy hats (guaranteed to be made in the U.S., not in China) to be delivered to our Eagle Susan Feldtman's living room in Houston. We passed them out to Convention Delegates and they absolutely loved them. Nobody rejected wearing a red hat.

We were very tolerant and let Delegates wear our hats even if they were not really pro-life because the hats looked so impressive on television. It soon looked like everybody was wearing a pro-life hat. We staged a news conference with many attractive young Republicans wearing the hats and admiring the fifty state boxes filled with pro-life pledges. At the appropriate time in the news conference, we rolled out a tremendous stream of signatures from Republican officeholders.

We were receiving about as much media as the pro-abortion crowd. Our new Republican National Coalition for Life became the sponsor of our event, and our sellout crowd filled the Houston Civic Center. Rush Limbaugh was our star speaker, backed up by other dignitaries such as Jerry Falwell and Vice President Dan Quayle.

The Subcommittee on Individual Rights, Good Homes and Safe Streets, chaired by Mary Potter Summa of North Carolina, conducted a dignified session with full debate, after which the vote was seventeen to three to retain the pro-life language of the 1984 Platform. The full Platform Committee then approved the pro-life Platform commitment by a vote of eighty-four to ten. On the first day of the Convention, the full Convention adopted the Platform by a unanimous voice vote.

After George H.W. Bush lost the 1992 election to Bill

Clinton, the media orchestrated a campaign to blame his defeat on the pro-lifers and those who had talked about the social issues, such as Pat Buchanan and Dan and Marilyn Quayle. However, the TV networks' own polls conducted right after the Convention reported that the Buchanan and Quayle speeches actually gave George Bush a big boost with the voters.

1996

Don't Change a Comma

At the 1996 Republican National Convention in San Diego, our goal was to retain the pro-life plank exactly as we had written it in 1984 in Dallas.

We adopted the slogan that we can't change a word "or a comma" because, if we did, that would give the media the opportunity to report that we had softened our solid pro-life position. Ann Stone was still hanging around.

As we geared up for the election, the media and the kingmakers launched a campaign to persuade Republican Delegates to nominate Colin Powell for President. But because he was a neophyte in political semantics, Powell made so many bloopers that his campaign rapidly ran aground. The worst was proclaiming himself "pro-choice."

So the kingmakers settled on Bob Dole even though

they were never really comfortable with him or his political tactics. Even the *New York Times* expressed bewilderment that Dole failed to campaign on any social issues or attack Clinton's veto of the very popular ban on partial-birth abortion. A *Times* front-page headline taunted him: "Dole Silent on Social Issues."

Colleen Parro was in constant touch with pro-life Republicans, encouraging them to elect the right people as National Delegates and especially to the Platform Committee. She trained them for political battles because we understood that our battle was political as well as moral and ideological.

Colleen Parro and I went to San Diego weeks before the Convention to select a headquarters and a place for our usual pro-life party. That's always a challenge because, months before a Convention meets, the Republican bigwigs lock up all the venues, all the hotels, and all the places where you can have parties, so that the Party controls everything in the city.

However, we were able to find a small hotel right across from the Convention Hall that was in bankruptcy, so it hadn't made it onto the Party's approved list. That's where we set up our headquarters. Pat Buchanan (for whom I was a delegate) and Gary Bauer, Chairman of the Family Research Council, were able to locate their headquarters there, too. At this San Diego Convention, we used white cowboy hats as our RNC for Life insignia.

Meanwhile, the pro-abortion Republicans were working very hard to water down the pro-life plank if they couldn't eliminate it altogether. When Arlen Specter announced his candidacy for President in 1996, he said his number-one goal was to get rid of the pro-life plank in the Republican Platform. Pete Wilson had just been reelected Governor of California with a larger majority than Reagan ever received, and he announced he was running for President on the number-one goal of taking pro-life language out of the Republican Platform. Again, we had very heavy ammunition aimed against our pro-life cause.

New Jersey Governor Christine Todd Whitman, who was widely predicted by TV pundits (such as John McLaughlin) as sure to get the Republican Vice-Presidential nomination in 1996 regardless of who was nominated for President, told a news conference on July 11, "The anti-abortion plank in the Republican Party Platform should be knocked out entirely. I don't even want to mess with modification, I just want it out of there."

Of course, pro-lifers wanted to have a "fun" party, so what's the biggest thing in San Diego? Shamu the whale, of course. I went to Sea World and made a deal for our party (with the whale) and signed the contract just thirty minutes before Republican officials discovered that venue. Our "Whale of a Party" at Sea World was another big success, attracting 1,300 people. Our star attraction, Shamu, performed on schedule.

Meanwhile, the kingmakers' candidate, Bob Dole, was steadily moving toward his nomination for President. That year, the chairman of the Platform Committee happened to be Congressman Henry Hyde, a lifelong personal and political friend of mine in Illinois and a nationally respected and articulate pro-life leader. That should have made our pro-life mission easy.

But there was one big problem: Henry Hyde was also a long-time buddy-buddy of Bob Dole and didn't want anything to harm Dole's election prospects as President.

Before every Republican Convention, we in RNC for Life would identify our true believers on the Platform Committee, and have a dinner for them ahead of time to plan our strategy. In San Diego, to make sure nobody could spy on us, we planned our caucus in a restaurant where we had to climb two steep flights of stairs (no elevator available).

Bob Dole was not easy to deal with. He wanted to get rid of the pro-life Platform plank because we were still in the era when Republican strategists were advising all candidates not to talk about social issues, especially about abortion. Dole wanted to purge the pro-life language altogether, but his "Plan B" was to add additional language to the Platform about promoting "tolerance." Our pro-lifers didn't want to say we're tolerant of abortion; that was not on our agenda.

During that summer of 1996, Dole shot himself in the foot several times. He had promised his pro-abortion supporters that he would either get rid of, or water down, the Party's pro-life plank. On June 10, Dole stated on CNN that a "tolerance" statement is "going to be in the abortion plank,"

37

adding, "I make that decision and it's not negotiable."

Dole apparently didn't know that the Presidential nominee could no longer dictate the Platform as Richard Nixon and Nelson Rockefeller dictated it in 1960. The Republican Platform Committee consists of one man and one woman elected from each state by all the members of their state's delegation. Republicans work hard to be elected, first as a delegate and then to the Platform Committee, so they take their responsibilities seriously.

I invited Platform Committee chairman Henry Hyde to attend our dinner at that little upstairs restaurant. I cordially introduced him, and then called on each Platform Delegate around the table to have a say about the pro-life plank. After we got halfway around the table, Congressman Hyde stood up and walked out. He realized that we were an "immovable rock," not willing to weaken our pro-life Platform commitment by any "tolerance" language.

Meanwhile, we were also working with Bob Dole's staff, whom Dole was checking with constantly, giving orders, getting information, and stating his demands. Finally, Dole's staff pulled the telephone plug out of the wall so they couldn't hear from him anymore.

The 1996 Platform Committee treated the pro-abortionists courteously and allowed them lengthy time to make their arguments, but the largest number of votes they received was 11 out of 107, a decline from the 16 they had received at the 1992 Convention in Houston. Eleven was not enough even to file a minority report.

Bob Dole then insulted the Delegates by announcing to the press, "I haven't read the platform and I'm not bound by it anyway." Dole's political strategists deleted the life, cultural, and sovereignty issues out of Dole's campaign. He then personally demanded that the following be added to the Party's Platform, and the weary committee included it: "We are the party of the open door ... we welcome into our ranks all those Americans who may hold differing positions." The committee humored Dole by including this, although it was obvious that he didn't believe it himself. Dole's convention managers soon made it crystal clear that the concepts of "open door," "diversity," welcoming "differing positions," "civility," and "mutual respect" applied only to the pro-abortion Rockefeller

Republicans – not to pro-lifers.

Despite the difficulties with Bob Dole, we won our Platform battle again. The Committee wrote a conservative, pro-life document that was unanimously adopted by the full convention on August 12. The key part of the 1996 Republican Platform was approved just as we wrote it in Dallas in 1984, and it did not include any Dole "tolerance" language. The pro-abortion crowd hung around in the halls but didn't have any influence. One of them complained to the press, "We are excluded, unwanted, untolerated, and unhappy."

The media labeled the winners in San Diego the "Fearsome Foursome" consisting of: Ralph Reed, executive director of the Christian Coalition; Bay Buchanan, sister of Pat; Gary Bauer, chairman of the Family Research Council; and me.

2000

Pro-Life Becomes the *Life* of the Party

T he next Convention was in 2000 in Philadelphia where, again, we had a fabulous RNC for Life party. Held at the Philadelphia Union League Club, it was another great success. The bitter pro-abortion feminists were picketing outside the Union League Club, but they were ignored. Our signature giveaway in Philadelphia was vests for all pro-life Delegates inscribed with the words, "The *Life* of the Party." That became our slogan; proclaiming that pro-lifers are truly "the *LIFE* of the Party."

The grassroots were so hungry to win back the White House after two terms of Bill Clinton that they were willing to tolerate Bush's deviations from conservative orthodoxy on many issues – but not on the sanctity of life. When the pro-abortion Governor of Pennsylvania, Tom Ridge, was floated as a possible running mate for Bush, pro-lifers quashed that bad idea by telling the *New York Times* that Bush would lose if he chose Ridge.

The 2000 Platform that we adopted was very strong both for life *and* for marriage. It read, "The unborn baby has a fundamental individual right to life" and "We support the traditional definition of marriage as the legal union of one man and one woman."

The pro-abortion minority in the Party staged its usual tantrums to get media coverage, but they were not successful in eliminating either the pro-life plank or the marriage plank in the Platform.

2004

Sticking By Our Principles

T he 2004 Republican National Convention was in New York City. Journalists were amazed at the tight control that the Bush Administration tried to exercise over the Platform Committee that year. One journalist commented that the Bush language dumped on the Platform Committee was kept as secret as the Manhattan Project and then handed down from on high like the Ten Commandments. Bush was praised on most of the 98 pages in the platform.

However, by 2004, it had become conventional wisdom that the Establishment had better not try to remove the pro-life language because we were determined to keep the plank just as we wrote it in 1984, word for word. We liked the language we had, and we didn't want it muddied up or watered down. We hosted our New York party at the Tavern on the Green featuring Ann Coulter and other valiant pro-lifers to whom we presented awards.

So Bush went along with the committee's retention of the same pro-life language that had been in the platform since 1984. Respect for the right to life of unborn babies has been official Republican Party doctrine ever since *Roe v. Wade,* and Republicans believe that the pro-life constituency is essential to political victories.

2008

Overcoming Unexpected Problems

B y the time we got to St. Paul, Minnesota, the 2008 Convention city, pro-life wasn't a big battle any more. Only a few disgruntled pro-aborts tried to continue the fight. We had established the Republican Party as *the* pro-life Party. It was now difficult for anybody to get a Republican nomination who didn't say he was pro-life. They may not have been as totally pro-life as many of us are, but nearly all Republican candidates now like to say they are pro-life.

RNC for Life had, and still has, a very detailed questionnaire that candidates are required to fill out if they want our endorsement.

Many months before the 2008 National Convention, we had signed up Alaska Governor Sarah Palin to be the featured speaker at our Republican National Coalition for Life

Luncheon. She was a rising star and we were confident she would be a big attraction for our pro-life event.

The day before our long-planned big RNC for Life event at the Crowne Plaza Hotel in St. Paul, the managers of the John McCain for President Campaign ordered Sarah Palin to cancel her appearance. After McCain named her as his Vice Presidential running mate, he didn't want her speaking to any event he didn't control.

You can imagine how hard that hit us; it would have absolutely destroyed the beautiful event we had been planning for six months. I worried that I would be expected to refund all the money we had received for tickets to this expensive event.

The good Lord came to our rescue. Suddenly the phone rang, and it was Laura Ingraham. She said, "I just arrived in St. Paul. Can I come to your party tomorrow?"

Welcome, Laura! Substituting for Sarah Palin, Laura Ingraham gave a tremendous speech, and nobody was disappointed.

One other event made that luncheon memorable. As our program started, I was introducing the dignitaries before I presented Laura Ingraham. Suddenly a troublemaker from a leftwing outfit called "Code Pink" rushed up on the stage carrying an obnoxious sign and tried to wrestle the microphone away from me. I fought her off until two Texans wearing cowboy hats came on the stage to rescue me. The audience loved the fight.

Our RNC for Life Event in St. Paul turned out to be one of our most memorable and successful.

2012

America Is Becoming Pro-Life

Pro-lifers are not only winning in the Republican Party; we're winning nationwide. Public opinion polls show that the majority of Americans now say they're pro-life. The whole country is coming our way and I am particularly cheered when I talk to young people. National public opinion polls confirm that young people are more pro-life than older people. It's very important that we keep on nominating candidates who are pro-life, and will vote pro-life and stick with us on the issues that are important to pro-life, such as the confirmation of judges.

It's been a tremendous fight, and RNC for Life together with Eagle Forum has led the battle. We have made it essential for Republican candidates to be pro-life. We are winning through the political process: nominating and electing candidates to public office; electing Delegates to the Republican National Conventions; and persuading Delegates on the Platform Committee to vote pro-life.

On January 22, 2014, the members of the entire Republican National Committee made history when they gathered in the lobby of the Renaissance Hotel in downtown Washington, DC. Buttoning up their coats on a winter day, each was handed a red baseball cap with RNC emblazoned across the front. This participation in the March for Life was arranged by the newly elected president of Eagle Forum, Ed Martin, and facilitated by Republican National Chairman Reince Priebus, who adjusted the agenda of a regular national RNC meeting to accommodate members' participation in the March for Life.

After a short bus ride across downtown to the Mall, they joined tens of thousands of Americans in the 41st annual March for Life, making a dramatic statement of how genuinely pro-life the Republican Party has become. Gone are the days when Republicans remained silent after an obviously wrong, unconstitutional and immoral decision by supremacist judges.

However, we are not ready to fold our tents and claim the battle for pro-life is over. The anti-life kingmakers and the high-paid strategists who advise our candidates, are still telling their clients and the recipients of their big campaign donations to avoid the moral and social issues.

The pro-life battle won't be over until we quash the unconstitutional push for judicial supremacy. It is clearly an un-American notion that one judge, or even a 5-to-4 majority of judges (none of whom is elected by the voters) can rewrite portions of our Constitution or declare that a human being (such as a baby in the womb) is the property of somebody else and can be killed by its alleged owner.

Our Constitution created a government of three co-equal branches, and certainly did not give the judicial branch the right to overrule the other branches.

In other words, pro-lifers can't celebrate victory until we expunge *Roe v. Wade* and *Doe v. Bolton* from having any constitutional authority or significance as a legal precedent.

We must assume that the pro-abortion faction, which has always been able to raise big bucks and prop up important people to speak for their cause, won't go away, but will be carrying on their mischief again at the 2016 Republican National Convention in Cleveland, Ohio. Pro-lifers must be in Cleveland in force to protect the tremendous gains we have made. This requires engaging in rough-and-tumble party politics in order to elect Delegates to that Convention who will retain the Republican position as the pro-life party.

2016

Trump's Pro-Life Party

The 2016 Republican Convention in Cleveland, Ohio was another roaring success for Phyllis Schlafly, the Republican icon. It was her 17th national Republican convention - she was there in 1952 for Senator Taft!

Phyllis was a master of working the Republican Party to get delegates selected or elected. We had a "56 state" strategy (50 states plus the six RNC-designated territories who had delegates) and gathered data on all the paths to Cleveland. We assisted folks in getting elected and when delegates were elected, we contacted them all by letter and email. We knew that the relationships we cultivated would bear fruit in Cleveland.

For more than a year beforehand at Phyllis' direction, we planned for the 2016 Republican Convention. Phyllis had weighed in against the RNC selecting Las Vegas for the convention site and was pleased they chose Cleveland, although she could be heard in the months before the Conventions joking: I'll see you in Cleveland in July - just what you were hoping for, I know, the summer in Cleveland!

In the Spring of 2016, Phyllis was elected by her fellow Missouri Republicans at the statewide convention to serve as one of Missouri's delegates—with Senator Roy Blunt instrumental in her election. Phyllis was honored to be asked to serve as Missouri's Platform Committee member but instead supported her long-time friend Bev Ehlen to serve with Hardy Billington on the important committee.

* * *

During her time in Cleveland, Phyllis attended every meeting of the Convention. She did scores of radio interviews on "radio row" and reveled in photographs with fellow Republicans. Watching Donald Trump receive the nomination was a high point.

Phyllis arrived in Cleveland on Saturday, July 9th and remained until Friday, July 21st. Her team arrived the days before her and stayed until the 23rd. Phyllis arrived by plane in

Cleveland on July 9th and departed the morning after Trump's July 21st acceptance speech. Two of our team, Ryan Hite and Jordan Henry drove in from St. Louis with equipment and other materials; their SUVs would prove indispensable for our operations during the two-week period.

Phyllis stayed at the Akron hotel with the Missouri delegation. She attended every session of the Convention and shuttled back and forth to do so. John Schlafly secured a floor pass and accompanied her. Phyllis took thousands of photos with friends and admirers and did scores of radio and TV interviews.

As Phyllis used to say "politics is where the action is" and this included socializing. One evening after a late Convention session, as Phyllis arrived back at the Akron hotel after midnight, Phyllis called Kathleen Sullivan and Priscilla Gray along with staff. "Meet me in the hotel restaurant," she instructed and proceeded to hold forth and debrief for another hour over a late night/early morning refreshment.

* * *

Once the RNC had selected Cleveland as host city, Phyllis sent members of her staff to Cleveland to scout locations for key work she knew we needed to accomplish. We needed 1) a home base, 2) the Platform Committee delegate dinner location, and 3) the site for the "Life of the Party" celebration hosted by Phyllis' RNC for Life organization. We found Cleveland very accommodating and found first-rate facilities.

1. Our home base was a rented home owned by a supporter of Phyllis, Jeanne Carney Hagan, who was kind enough to allow its use and even to decorate as we needed. In a leafy, historic section near downtown, 1138 Edgewater Drive became our buzzing HQ for staff, operations, and where Phyllis took private meetings to strategize. Located about 4 miles from the Convention site, the home was a meeting place, a dormitory, and general a hub for our activity. Rebekah Gantner, Phyllis' long-time executive director, supervised the work. Two Eagle interns, Sean Delaney and Jordan Henry, worked out of there along with Communications Director Ryan Hite. An amazing Clevelander named Sharon Deitrick was responsible for much of our accommodations and contributed to our success.

During the nearly two weeks in Cleveland, we hosted guests like Andy Schlafly and Ned Pfeifer, Phyllis' cousin and our PA Eagle leader. Conservative leaders stopped by for meals and coffee or just to check in. We supplied thousands of convention attendees with books and other materials which were kept in storage at the Edgewater residence.

2. On Sunday July 10th, Phyllis hosted her regular delegate training dinner in a private room at the Alley Cat restaurant in the Flats East Bank District over-looking the Cuyahoga River. The delegate dinner was held in the same room that LeBron James used just a few days before to celebrate the Cleveland Cavaliers NBA championship.

More than 80 people attended the dinner and heard speakers address key delegate issues especially regarding the Platform Committee. California delegate and long-time friend of Phyllis Andy Puzder promised to take a leadership role on the Platform Committee. Michigan delegate and Platform Committee member Meshawn Maddock asked numerous questions about the Con-Con issue—promising to fight against any effort to put it in the Platform.

The dinner went for nearly 4 hours and accomplished the goals set by Phyllis: train the delegates and network to be ready to assist over the next four days when the Platform and other Convention rules would be adopted.

3. RNC for Life hosted its quadrennial "Life of the Party" on Tuesday, July 19, 2016 at the home of the Cleveland Browns—FirstEnergy Stadium. The noon lunch was themed "Fight for Life" and included speaker and former Notre Dame Coach Lou Holtz as well as coaching legend Gerry Faust. Cleveland Auxiliary Bishop Roger Gries, OSB led the more than 435 lifers in prayer and long-time friend of Phyllis Ralph Reed gave a stemwinder. Media from all over the world covered the lunch and Eagle leader and head of the Utah Eagles Cherilyn Eagar broadcast the luncheon program in person and live on KTalk radio, her Utah radio home.

* * *

Phyllis believed in the Republican Platform and she was always thinking about how to strengthen it and protect it.

57

At her March 11, 2016 meeting with Donald Trump just moments before Phyllis endorsed him at the Peabody Opera House in downtown St. Louis, Missouri, Phyllis asked Trump for his help. She sought and received Trump's specific assurance that he would defend the conservative Republican Platform that Phyllis had worked so hard to craft. In Cleveland, Trump and his staff lived up to his word.

The Platform adopted at the 2016 Convention may be the most conservative one we have ever had. Protection for life and for family were included. Silly last minute efforts to add a call for a Constitutional Convention were defeated. Military superiority was included. It is a great Platform for a great candidate.

Phyllis completed her last Convention with a sense of pride and relief: her Republican Party was strong and its nominee was on his way to the Presidency.

* * *

Rejecting Judicial Supremacy

T he Republican Party was born on the principle that no human being should be considered the property of another. That is our heritage as Republicans.

The most famous political debates in American history were the Lincoln-Douglas Debates of 1858. During those seven debates up and down the State of Illinois, Abraham Lincoln enunciated the position of the then-new Republican Party that slavery was "a moral, a social and a political wrong," and that he "looks forward to a time when slavery shall be abolished everywhere."

The Democratic candidate, Stephen A. Douglas, argued that the Supreme Court's ruling in *Dred Scott v. Sandford* had settled the slavery question once and for all. Saying, "I choose to abide by the decisions of the Supreme Court as they are pronounced," Douglas argued that everyone was bound to accept the Court's decision that the U.S. Constitution protects an individual property right in slaves throughout the United

States and its Western territories.

Abraham Lincoln did not dispute the authority of the Supreme Court to decide a particular case, but he forthrightly proclaimed, "We do not propose to be bound by it as a political rule. We propose to have it reversed if we can, and a new judicial rule established upon this subject."

Lincoln thus rejected *judicial supremacy*, the notion that major constitutional decisions can be made by what he called "that eminent tribunal" instead of by "we the people."

In Quincy, Illinois, Lincoln argued that we should "deal with [slavery] as with any other wrong, insofar as we can prevent its growing any larger, and deal with it that, in the run of time, there may be some promise of an end to it. We have a due regard to the actual presence of it amongst us and the difficulties of getting rid of it in any satisfactory way … [but] we oppose it as an evil."

As authority for saying that slavery was "wrong," Lincoln cited our nation's founding document, the Declaration of Independence, which asserts as a "self-evident" truth that each of us is "endowed by their Creator" with unalienable rights of life and liberty, and that government is instituted for the purpose of securing those rights.

"The real issue in this controversy," Lincoln said in the Alton, Illinois, debate, is that the Republican Party "looks upon the institution of slavery as a wrong" and the Democratic Party "does not look upon it as a wrong." Lincoln proclaimed that the slavery issue represented "the eternal struggle between these two principles – right and wrong."

In reporting the Lincoln-Douglas debates, the biased press of the 1850s called Lincoln "a dead dog" walking to his "political grave," and reported Stephen Douglas' arguments as "logical" and "powerful." Lincoln lost that Senatorial election to Douglas. But two years later, in a rematch against Senator Douglas, Abraham Lincoln was elected our first Republican President – and the verdict of history is on Lincoln's side.

Abortion is the right-or-wrong issue of our time. We should parallel the words of Abraham Lincoln today and say, "The Republican Party looks upon abortion as a wrong, and the Democratic Party does not look upon it as a wrong." That's the crucial difference between the two parties.

Republicans must not adopt the Stephen Douglas position that a wrong Supreme Court decision is infallible and irrevocable. We must repudiate the 1973 Supreme Court decision in *Roe v. Wade*, which legalized the deliberate killing of unborn babies.

The Declaration of Independence does not mention abortion, but you will search in vain for a single affirmation that the Creator-endowed right to life was to be withheld from a baby until the moment of birth. Every new advance in science, especially the DNA and the ultra-sound photographs of babies in the womb, confirms that the unique, individual identity of each of us is present, human, alive and growing even before the mother realizes she is pregnant.

The Republican Party's position as the pro-life party was arrived at through the democratic process and maintained consistently through ten Republican National Conventions and Platforms in 1976, 1980, 1984, 1988, 1992, 1996, 2000, 2004, 2008, and 2012. A Party Platform is a standard, a banner to raise on high, to proclaim our general principles and display our convictions. It is not legislation. Our Platform is strong on strategic principle, while leaving details and tactics to the legislative process.

The Republican Party was founded on the principle that no human being should be considered the property of another, and on a repudiation of a U.S. Supreme Court which had ruled otherwise.

We reject rule by supremacist judges who espouse heretical notions that our U.S. Constitution is a "living" or "evolving" document that Supreme Court justices can amend or rewrite. We call for a return to government by "we the people" expressing their will through our three co-equal branches of government. When supremacist judges presume to rewrite portions of our law, most especially if it is a law that we have had for millennia such as our law defining marriage, it's time for the American people to speak up and say "No" just as Abe Lincoln did when supremacist judges ruled that blacks could be considered another man's "property."

On March 8, 2004 President Bush delivered this

challenge: "We will not stand for judges who undermine democracy by legislating from the bench and try to remake the culture of America by court order." Every presidential candidate should be asked to repeat that pledge.

What kind of a country do we want America to be? Do we want a country where "we the people" are sovereign, where we are governed by legislators we elect, where we can continue to raise our children in a land where the government respects our religious, cultural and family rights? Or will we allow ourselves to be ruled by an unelected cadre of judges?

All those who love liberty must oppose judicial supremacy and its advocates. In the words of the Declaration of Independence, we must disavow these "usurpations."

Likewise in the marriage case, we reject the notion that an unelected judge can rewrite our definition of marriage that has been a part of our law and culture for millennia. All Americans must use every tool in the political process to reject judicial supremacy and return to government by "we the people."

Afterword

Over the past few years I have given hundreds of talks on college campuses and spoken to thousands of young people. I have learned that an important lesson that I can give these young students for life is this: victory is possible and that the hard fought battles are the ones worth fighting.

Phyllis Schlafly is a hero of mine – and of many people for many reasons. She is a clear and persuasive writer of more than 25 books and thousands of columns. She is a classy woman who delivers powerful speeches. I have been impressed by her career of service, her ability to build a national organization, and her joy in fighting the good fight.

What you have just read is the heretofore untold story of how a band of pro-lifers went about changing the course of American history by changing the Republican Party. After the 1973 Roe v. Wade abortion decision, Phyllis and those early pro-lifers refused to accept the conventional wisdom – offered by national Republican leaders as well as media pundits – that the "Supreme Court has spoken, it's the law of the land, and folks need to get over it and move on."

Phyllis rejected this advice and built a pro-life army who set about making the Republican Party pro-life. They started with a pro-life plank in the Republican platform. Phyllis started RNC for Life, a pro-life organization focused on supporting pro-life Republicans. Over the decades, Phyllis and her army defended the pro-life plank and grew the size and strength of their membership. Today, there is no national Republican candidate who dares be anything other than pro-life!

If you care about winning, this book helps us understand how to win. If you care about inspiring others, this book shows us how to emulate Phyllis. More than anything if you care to know why America is great and why her people will always step up for the true and good fights, this book clearly declares what is behind a core value of the Republican Party today, and of our nation.

After reading this book, I hope that you can now see clearly why Phyllis Schlafly is a great American hero.

Kristan Hawkins
President, Students for Life of America

Appendix A
Historic Pro-Life References
in Republican Platforms

1976

The American Family

Families must continue to be the foundation of our nation.

Families—not government programs—are the best way to make sure our children are properly nurtured, our elderly are cared for, our cultural and spiritual heritages are perpetuated, our laws are observed and our values are preserved.

Because of our concern for family values, we affirm our beliefs, stated elsewhere in this Platform, in many elements that will make our country a more hospitable environment for family life—neighborhood schools; educational systems that include and are responsive to parents' concerns; estate tax changes to establish more realistic exemptions which will minimize disruption of already bereaved families; a position on abortion that values human life; a welfare policy to encourage rather than discourage families to stay together and seek economic independence; a tax system that assists rather than penalizes families with elderly members, children in day care or children in college; economic and employment policies that stop the shrinkage of our dollars and stimulate the creation of jobs so that families can plan for their economic security.

While we support valid medical and biological research efforts which can produce life-saving results, we oppose any research on live fetuses. We are also opposed to any legislation which sanctions ending the life of any patient.

We protest the Supreme Court's intrusion into the family structure through its denial of the parents' obligation and right to guide their minor children. The Republican Party favors a continuance of the public dialogue on abortion and supports the efforts of those who seek enactment of a constitutional amendment to restore protection of the right to life for unborn children.

1980

Abortion

There can be no doubt that the question of abortion, despite the complex nature of its various issues, is ultimately concerned with equality of rights under the law. While we recognize differing views on this question among Americans in general—and in our own Party—we affirm our support of a constitutional amendment to restore protection of the right to life for unborn children. We also support the Congressional efforts to restrict the use of taxpayers' dollars for abortion.

1984

Our Constitutional System

The unborn child has a fundamental individual right to life which cannot be infringed. We therefore reaffirm our support for a human life amendment to the Constitution, and we endorse legislation to make clear that the Fourteenth Amendment's protections apply to unborn children. We oppose the use of public revenues for abortion and will eliminate funding for organizations which advocate or support abortion.

We commend the efforts of those individuals and religious and private organizations that are providing positive alternatives to abortion by meeting the physical, emotional, and financial needs of pregnant women and offering adoption services where needed.

We applaud President Reagan's fine record of judicial appointments, and we reaffirm our support for the appointment of judges at all levels of the judiciary who respect traditional family values and the sanctity of innocent human life.

1988

Constitutional Government and Individual Rights

The unborn child has a fundamental individual right to life which cannot be infringed. We therefore reaffirm our support for a human life amendment to the Constitution, and we endorse legislation to make clear that the Fourteenth Amendment's protections apply to unborn children. We oppose the use of public revenues for abortion and will eliminate funding for organizations which advocate or support abortion. We commend the efforts of those individuals and religious and private organizations that are providing positive alternatives to abortion by meeting the physical, emotional, and financial needs of pregnant women and offering adoption services where needed.

We applaud President Reagan's fine record of judicial appointments, and we reaffirm our support for the appointment of judges at all levels of the judiciary who respect traditional family values and the sanctity of innocent human life.

Values are the core of good education. A free society needs a moral foundation for its learning. We oppose any programs in public schools which provide birth control or abortion services or referrals. Our "first line of defense" to protect our youth from contracting AIDS and other sexually communicable diseases, from teen pregnancy, and from illegal drug use must be abstinence education.

1992

Individual Rights

The protection of individual rights is the foundation for opportunity and security.

… We believe the unborn child has a fundamental individual right to life which cannot be infringed. We therefore reaffirm our support for a human life amendment to the Constitution, and we endorse legislation to make clear that the Fourteenth Amendment's protections apply to unborn children. We oppose using public revenues for abortion and will not fund organizations which advocate it. We commend those who provide alternatives to abortion by meeting the needs of mothers and offering adoption services. We reaffirm our support for appointment of judges who respect traditional family values and the sanctity of innocent human life.

… Accordingly, we oppose programs in public schools that provide birth control or abortion services or referrals. Instead, we encourage abstinence education programs with proven track records in protecting youth from disease, pregnancy, and drug use.

... Because we uphold the family as the building block of economic progress, we protect its rights in international programs and will continue to withhold funds from organizations involved in abortion.

1996

Principles

... Because institutions like the family are the backbone of a healthy society, we believe government must support the rights of the family; and recognizing within our own ranks different approaches toward our common goal, we reaffirm respect for the sanctity of human life.

The unborn child has a fundamental individual right to life which cannot be infringed. We support a human life amendment to the Constitution and we endorse legislation to make clear that the Fourteenth Amendment's protections apply to unborn children. Our purpose is to have legislative and judicial protection of that right against those who perform abortions. We oppose using public revenues for abortion and will not fund organizations which advocate it. We support the appointment of judges who respect traditional family values and the sanctity of innocent human life.

Our goal is to ensure that women with problem pregnancies have the kind of support, material and otherwise, they need for themselves and for their babies, not to be punitive towards those for whose difficult situation we have only compassion. We oppose abortion, but our pro-life agenda does not include punitive action against women who have an abortion. We salute those who provide alternatives to abortion and offer adoption services. Republicans in Congress took the lead in expanding assistance both for the costs of adoption and for the continuing care of adoptive children with special needs.

Human nature and aspirations are the same everywhere, and everywhere the family is the building block of economic and social progress. We therefore will protect the rights of families in international programs and will not fund organizations involved in abortion.

Abstinence education in the home will lead to less need for birth control services and fewer abortions. We support educational initiatives to promote chastity until marriage as the expected standard of behavior. This education initiative is the best preventive measure to avoid the emotional trauma of sexually-transmitted diseases and teen pregnancies that are serious problems among our young people. While recognizing that something must be done to help children when parental consent or supervision is not possible, we oppose school-based clinics, which provide referrals, counseling, and related services for contraception and abortion.

2000

Upholding the Rights of All

The Supreme Court's recent decision, prohibiting states from banning partial-birth abortions—a procedure denounced by a committee of the American Medical Association and rightly branded as four-fifths infanticide—shocks the conscience of the nation. As a country, we must keep our pledge to the first guarantee of the Declaration of Independence. That is why we say the unborn child has a fundamental individual right to life which cannot be infringed. We support a human life amendment to the Constitution and we endorse legislation to make clear that the Fourteenth Amendment's protections apply to unborn children. Our purpose is to have legislative and judicial protection of that right against those who perform abortions. We oppose using public revenues for abortion and will not fund organizations which advocate it. We support the appointment of judges who respect traditional family values and the sanctity of innocent human life.

Our goal is to ensure that women with problem pregnancies have the kind of support, material and otherwise, they need for themselves and for their babies, not to be punitive towards those for whose difficult situation we have only compassion. We oppose abortion, but our pro-life agenda does not include punitive action against women who have an abortion. We salute those who provide alternatives to abortion and offer adoption services, and we commend congressional Republicans for expanding assistance to adopting families and for removing racial barriers to adoption.

Children At Risk

... We renew our call for replacing "family planning" programs for teens with increased funding for abstinence education, which teaches abstinence until marriage as the responsible and expected standard of behavior.

The United Nations

The United Nations was created to benefit all peoples and nations, not to promote a radical agenda of social engineering. Any effort to address global social problems must be firmly placed into a context of respect for the fundamental social institutions of marriage and family. We reject any treaty or convention that would contradict these values. For that reason, we will protect the rights of families in international programs and will not fund organizations involved in abortion.

2004

International Institutions

Any effort to address global social problems must be firmly placed within a context of respect for the fundamental social institutions of marriage and family. We reject any treaty or convention that would contradict these values. For that reason, we support protecting the rights of families in international programs and oppose funding organizations involved in abortion.

Supporting Judges Who Uphold the Law

In the federal courts, scores of judges with activist backgrounds in the hard-left now have lifetime tenure. Recent events have made it clear that these judges threaten America's dearest institutions and our very way of life. In some states, activist judges are redefining the institution of marriage. While the vast majority of Americans support a ban on partial-birth abortion, this brutal and violent practice will likely continue by judicial fiat. We believe that the self-proclaimed supremacy of these judicial activists is antithetical to the democratic ideals on which our nation was founded.

Promoting Healthy Choices, Including Abstinence

We oppose school-based clinics that provide referrals, counseling, and related services for contraception and abortion.

Promoting a Culture of Life

As a country, we must keep our pledge to the first guarantee of the Declaration of Independence. That is why we say the unborn child has a fundamental individual right to life which cannot be infringed. We support a human life amendment to the Constitution and we endorse legislation to make it clear that the Fourteenth Amendment's protections apply to unborn children. Our purpose is to have legislative and judicial protection of that right against those who perform abortions. We oppose using public revenues for abortion and will not fund organizations which advocate it. We support the appointment of judges who respect traditional family values and the sanctity of innocent human life.

2008

Maintaining The Sanctity and Dignity of Human Life

At its core, abortion is a fundamental assault on the sanctity of innocent human life. Women deserve better than abortion. Every effort should be made to work with women considering abortion to enable and empower them to choose life. We salute those who provide them alternatives, including pregnancy care centers.

Securing the Peace - Sovereign American Leadership in International Organizations

… Because the UN has no mandate to promote radical social engineering, any effort to address global social problems must respect the fundamental institutions of marriage and family. We assert the rights of families in all international programs and will not fund organizations involved in abortion. We strongly support the long-held policy of the Republican Party known as the "Mexico City policy," which prohibits federal monies from being given to non-governmental organizations that provide abortions or actively promote abortion as a method of family planning in other countries. We reject any treaty or agreement that would violate those values.

Patient Control and Portability

Because the family is our basic unit of society, we fully support parental rights to consent to medical treatment for their children including mental health treatment, drug treatment, alcohol treatment, and treatment involving pregnancy, contraceptives and abortion.

Principles for Elementary and Secondary Education

We renew our call for replacing "family planning" programs for teens with increased funding for abstinence education, which teaches abstinence until marriage as the responsible and expected standard of behavior. Abstinence from sexual activity is the only protection that is 100 percent effective against out-of-wedlock pregnancies and sexually transmitted diseases, including HIV/AIDS when transmitted sexually. We oppose school-based clinics that provide referrals, counseling, and related services for abortion and contraception. Schools should not ask children to answer offensive or intrusive personal nonacademic questionnaires without parental consent.

2012

The Sanctity and Dignity of Human Life

Faithful to the "self-evident" truths enshrined in the Declaration of Independence, we assert the sanctity of human life and affirm that the unborn child has a fundamental individual right to life which cannot be infringed. We support a human life amendment to the Constitution and endorse legislation to make clear that the Fourteenth Amendment's protections apply to unborn children. We oppose using public revenues to promote or perform abortion or fund organizations which perform or advocate it and will not fund or subsidize health care which includes abortion coverage. We support the appointment of judges who respect traditional family values and the sanctity of innocent human life.

Republican leadership has led the effort to prohibit the barbaric practice of partial-birth abortion and permitted States to extend health care coverage to children before birth. We urge Congress to strengthen the Born Alive Infant Protection Act by enacting appropriate civil and criminal penalties on healthcare providers who fail to provide treatment and care to an infant who survives an abortion, including early induction delivery where the death of the infant is intended. We call for legislation to ban sex-selective abortions—gender discrimination in its most lethal form—and to protect from abortion unborn children who are capable of feeling pain; and we applaud U.S. House Republicans for leading the effort to protect the lives of pain-capable unborn children in the District of Columbia. We call for a ban on the use of body parts from aborted fetuses for research. We support and applaud adult stem cell research to develop lifesaving therapies, and we oppose the killing of embryos for their stem cells. We oppose federal funding of embryonic stem cell research.

We also salute the many States that have passed laws for informed consent, mandatory waiting periods prior to an abortion, and health-protective clinic regulation. We seek to protect young girls from exploitation through a parental consent requirement; and we affirm our moral obligation to assist, rather than penalize, women challenged by an unplanned pregnancy. We salute those who provide them with counseling and adoption alternatives and empower them to choose life, and we take comfort in the tremendous increase in adoptions that has followed Republican legislative initiatives.

Appendix B

Excerpts from the

2016 Republican Platform

With this platform, we the Republican Party reaffirm the principles that unite us in a common purpose.

We believe in American exceptionalism.

We believe the United States of America is unlike any other nation on earth.

We believe America is exceptional because of our historic role—first as refuge, then as defender, and now as exemplar of liberty for the world to see.

We affirm—as did the Declaration of Independence: that all are created equal, endowed by their Creator with inalienable rights of life, liberty, and the pursuit of happiness.

We believe in the Constitution as our founding document.

We believe the Constitution was written not as a flexible document, but as our enduring covenant.

We believe our constitutional system—limited government, separation of powers, federalism, and the rights of the people— must be preserved uncompromised for future generations.

We believe political freedom and economic freedom are indivisible.

When political freedom and economic freedom are separated— both are in peril; when united, they are invincible. We believe that people are the ultimate resource—and that the people, not the government, are the best stewards of our country's God-given natural resources.

As Americans and as Republicans we wish for peace — so we insist on strength. We will make America safe. We seek friendship with all peoples and all nations, but we recognize and are prepared to deal with evil in the world.

Based on these principles, this platform is an invitation and a roadmap. It invites every American to join us and shows the path to a stronger, safer, and more prosperous America.

This platform is optimistic because the American people are optimistic.

This platform lays out—in clear language—the path to making America great and united again.

For the past eight years America has been led in the wrong direction.

Our economy has become unnecessarily weak with stagnant wages. People living paycheck to paycheck are struggling, sacrificing, and suffering.

Americans have earned and deserve a strong and healthy economy.

Our standing in world affairs has declined significantly—our enemies no longer fear us and our friends no long trust us.

People want and expect an America that is the most powerful and respected country on the face of the earth.

The men and women of our military remain the world's best. The have been shortchanged in numbers, equipment, and benefits by a Commander in Chief who treats the Armed Forces and our veterans as a necessary inconvenience.

The President and the Democratic party have dismantled Americans' system of healthcare. They have replaced it with a costly and complicated scheme that limits choices and takes away our freedom.

The President and the Democratic party have abandoned their promise of being accountable to the American people. They have nearly doubled the size of the national debt. They refuse to control our borders but try to control our schools, farms, businesses, and even our religious institutions. They have directly attacked the production of American energy and the industry-related jobs that have sustained families and communities.

The President has been regulating to death a free market economy that he does not like and does not understand. He defies the laws of the United States by refusing to enforce those with which he does not agree. And he appoints judges who legislate from the bench rather than apply the law.

We, as Republicans and Americans, cannot allow this to continue. That is why the many sections of this platform affirm our trust in the people, our faith in their judgment, and our determination to help them take back their country.

This means removing the power from unelected, unaccountable government.

This means relieving the burden and expense of punishing government regulations.

And this means returning to the people and the states the control that belongs to them. It is the control and the power to make their own decisions about what's best for themselves and their families and communities.

This platform is many things: A handbook for returning decision-making to the people. A guide to the constitutional rights of every American. And a manual for the kind of sustained growth that will bring opportunity to all those on the sidelines of our society.

Every time we sing, "God Bless America," we are asking for help. We ask for divine help that our country can fulfill its promise. We earn that help by recommitting ourselves to the ideas and ideals that are the true greatness of America.

Senator John Barrasso, Chairman
Governor Mary Fallin, Co-Chair
Representative Virginia Foxx, Co-Chair

REBIRTH OF A CONSTITUTIONAL GOVERNMENT

We the People

We are the party of the Declaration of Independence and the Constitution. The Declaration sets forth the fundamental precepts of American government: That God bestows certain inalienable rights on every individual, thus producing human equality; that government exists first and foremost to protect those inalienable rights; that man-made law must be consistent with God-given, natural rights; and that if God-given, natural, inalienable rights come in conflict with government, court, or human-granted rights, God-given, natural, inalienable rights always prevail; that there is a moral law recognized as "the Laws of Nature and of Nature's God"; and that American government is to operate with the consent of the governed. We are also the party of the Constitution, the greatest political document ever written. It is the solemn compact built upon principles of the Declaration that enshrines our God-given individual rights and ensures that all Americans stand equal before the law, defines the purposes and limits of government, and is the blueprint for ordered liberty that makes the United States the world's freest and most prosperous nation.

We reaffirm the Constitution's fundamental principles: limited government, separation of powers, individual liberty, and the rule of law. We denounce bigotry, racism, anti-Semitism, ethnic prejudice, and religious intolerance. Therefore, we oppose discrimination based on race, sex, religion, creed, disability, or national origin and support statutes to end such discrimination. As the Party of Abraham Lincoln, we must continue to foster solutions to America's difficult challenges when it comes to race relations today. We continue to encourage equality for all citizens and access to the American Dream. Merit and hard work should determine advancement in our society, so we reject unfair preferences, quotas, and set-asides as forms of discrimination. Our ranks include Americans from every faith and tradition, and we respect the right of each American to follow his or her deeply held beliefs.

Our Constitution is in crisis. More than 90 percent of federal requirements are now imposed by regulatory agencies, without any vote of the House or Senate or signature of the President. The current Administration has exceeded its constitutional authority, brazenly and flagrantly violated the separation of powers, sought to divide America into groups and turn citizen against citizen. The President has refused to defend or enforce laws he does not like, used executive orders to enact national policies in areas constitutionally reserved solely to Congress, made unconstitutional "recess" appointments to Senate-confirmed positions, directed regulatory agencies to overstep their statutory authority, and failed to consult Congress regarding military action overseas. He has changed what John Adams called "a government of laws and not of men" into just the opposite.

Democrats in Congress have enabled, supported, and defended each of these breaches. They have applauded the President's efforts to do an end-run around Congress and stymied Republican efforts to restrain executive lawlessness. Democrats in Congress have also endorsed an anti-constitutional agenda of their own. Forty-eight Democratic senators, for instance, voted to amend the Bill of Rights to give government officials control over political speech. Democrats in Congress have likewise proposed bills that would limit religious liberty, undermine property rights, and eviscerate the Second Amendment.

In a free society, the primary role of government is to protect the God-given, inalienable rights of its citizens. These constitutional rights are not negotiable for any American. We affirm that all legislation, regulation, and official actions must conform to the Constitution's original meaning as understood at the time the language was adopted. Our most urgent task as a Party is to restore the American people's faith in their government by electing a president who will enforce duly enacted laws, honor constitutional limits on executive authority, and return credibility to the Oval Office. We need a Republican president who will end abuses of power by departments and agencies, like the IRS and the EPA, and by the White House itself. Safeguarding our liberties requires a president who will respect the Constitution's separation of powers, including the authority of Congress to write legislation and define agency authority. Americans also deserve a president who will speak for our nation's history and values, not apologize for them to our enemies.

The Judiciary

The rule of law is the foundation of our Republic. A critical
threat to our country's constitutional order is an activist
judiciary that usurps powers properly reserved to the people
through other branches of government. Only a Republican
president will appoint judges who respect the rule of law
expressed within the Constitution and Declaration of
Independence, including the inalienable right to life and the
laws of nature and nature's God, as did the late Justice Antonin
Scalia. We are facing a national crisis in our judiciary. We
understand that only by electing a Republican president in
2016 will America have the opportunity for up to five new
constitutionally-minded Supreme Court justices appointed to
fill vacancies on the Court. Only such appointments will enable
courts to begin to reverse the long line of activist decisions—
including Roe, Obergefell, and the Obamacare cases—that
have usurped Congress's and states' lawmaking authority,
undermined constitutional protections, expanded the power of
the judiciary at the expense of the people and their elected
representatives, and stripped the people of their power to
govern themselves. We believe in the constitutional checks and
balances and that the Founders intended the judiciary to be the

weakest branch. We encourage Congress to use the check of impeachment for judges who unconstitutionally usurp Article I powers. In tandem with a Republican Senate, a new Republican president will restore to the Court a strong conservative majority that will follow the text and original meaning of the Constitution and our laws.

The legitimate powers of government are rooted in the consent of the American people. Judicial activism that includes reliance on foreign law or unratified treaties undermines American sovereignty. Foreign laws and precedents should not be used to interpret our Constitution or laws, nor should foreign sources of law be used in state courts' adjudication of criminal or civil matters.

We also affirm the wisdom of President George Washington's warning to avoid foreign entanglements and unnecessary alliances. We therefore oppose the adoption or ratification of treaties that would weaken or encroach upon American sovereignty or that could be construed by courts to do so. We will not recognize as binding upon the United States any international agreement forged without the constitutionally required assent of two-thirds of the United States Senate.

Defending Marriage Against an Activist Judiciary

Traditional marriage and family, based on marriage between one man and one woman, is the foundation for a free society and has for millennia been entrusted with rearing children and instilling cultural values. We condemn the Supreme Court's ruling in United States v. Windsor, which wrongly removed the ability of Congress to define marriage policy in federal law. We also condemn the Supreme Court's lawless ruling in Obergefell v. Hodges, which in the words of the late Justice Antonin Scalia, was a "judicial Putsch" — full of "silly extravagances" — that reduced "the disciplined legal reasoning of John Marshall and Joseph Storey to the mystical aphorisms of a fortune cookie." In Obergefell, five unelected lawyers robbed 320 million Americans of their legitimate constitutional authority to define marriage as the union of one man and one woman. The Court twisted the meaning of the Fourteenth Amendment beyond recognition. To echo Scalia, we dissent. We, therefore, support the appointment of justices and judges who respect the constitutional limits on their power and respect the authority of the states to decide such fundamental social questions.

The First Amendment: Religious Liberty

The Bill of Rights lists religious liberty, with its rights of conscience, as the first freedom to be protected. Religious freedom in the Bill of Rights protects the right of the people to practice their faith in their everyday lives. As George Washington taught, "religion and morality are indispensable supports" to a free society. Similarly, Thomas Jefferson declared that "No provision in our Constitution ought to be dearer to man than that which protects the rights of conscience against the enterprises of the civil authority." Ongoing attempts to compel individuals, businesses, and institutions of faith to transgress their beliefs are part of a misguided effort to undermine religion and drive it from the public square. As a result, many charitable religious institutions that have demonstrated great success in helping the needy have been barred from receiving government grants and contracts. Government officials threaten religious colleges and universities with massive fines and seek to control their personnel decisions. Places of worship for the first time in our history have reason to fear the loss of tax-exempt status merely for espousing and practicing traditional religious beliefs that have been held across the world for thousands of years, and for

97

almost four centuries in America. We value the right of America's religious leaders to preach, and Americans to speak freely, according to their faith. Republicans believe the federal government, specifically the IRS, is constitutionally prohibited from policing or censoring speech based on religious convictions or beliefs, and therefore we urge the repeal of the Johnson Amendment.

We pledge to defend the religious beliefs and rights of conscience of all Americans and to safeguard religious institutions against government control. We endorse the First Amendment Defense Act, Republican legislation in the House and Senate which will bar government discrimination against individuals and businesses for acting on the belief that marriage is the union of one man and one woman. This Act would protect the non-profit tax status of faith-based adoption agencies, the accreditation of religious educational institutions, the grants and contracts of faith-based charities and small businesses, and the licensing of religious professions—all of which are under assault by elements of the Democratic Party. We encourage every state to pass similar legislation. We likewise endorse the efforts of Republican state legislators and governors who have defied intimidation from corporations and the media in defending religious liberty. We support laws to confirm the longstanding American tradition that religious individuals and institutions can educate young people, receive government benefits, and participate in public debates without having to check their religious beliefs at the door.

Our First Amendment rights are not given to us by the government but are rights we inherently possess. The government cannot use subsequent amendments to limit First Amendment rights. The Free Exercise Clause is both an individual and a collective liberty protecting a right to worship God according to the dictates of conscience. Therefore, we strongly support the freedom of Americans to act in accordance with their religious beliefs, not only in their houses of worship, but also in their everyday lives.

We support the right of the people to conduct their businesses in accordance with their religious beliefs and condemn public officials who have proposed boycotts against businesses that support traditional marriage. We pledge to protect those business owners who have been subjected to hate campaigns, threats of violence, and other attempts to deny their civil rights.

We support the public display of the Ten Commandments as a reflection of our history and our country's Judeo-Christian heritage and further affirm the rights of religious students to engage in voluntary prayer at public school events and to have equal access to school facilities. We assert the First Amendment right of freedom of association for religious, private, service, and youth organizations to set their own membership standards.

The First Amendment: Constitutionally Protected Speech

The rights of citizenship do not stop at the ballot box. Freedom of speech includes the right to devote resources to whatever cause or candidate one supports. We oppose any restrictions or conditions that would discourage citizens from participating in the public square or limit their ability to promote their ideas, such as requiring private organizations to publicly disclose their donors to the government. Limits on political speech serve only to protect the powerful and insulate incumbent officeholders. We support repeal of federal restrictions on political parties in McCain-Feingold, raising or repealing contribution limits, protecting the political speech of advocacy groups, corporations, and labor unions, and protecting political speech on the internet. We likewise call for an end to the so-called Fairness Doctrine, and support free-market approaches to free speech unregulated by government.

We believe the forced funding of political candidates through union dues and other mandatory contributions violates the First Amendment. Just as Americans have a First Amendment right to devote resources to favored candidates or views, they have a First Amendment right not to be forced to individually support individuals or ideologies that they oppose. We agree with Thomas Jefferson that, "To compel a man to furnish contributions of money for the propagation of opinions which he disbelieves and abhors is sinful and tyrannical."

The Second Amendment: Our Right to Keep & Bear Arms

We uphold the right of individuals to keep and bear arms, a natural inalienable right that predates the Constitution and is secured by the Second Amendment. Lawful gun ownership enables Americans to exercise their God-given right of self-defense for the safety of their homes, their loved ones, and their communities.

We salute the Republican Congress for defending the right to keep and bear arms by preventing the President from installing a new liberal majority on the Supreme Court. The confirmation to the Court of additional anti-gun justices would eviscerate the Second Amendment's fundamental protections. Already, local officials in the nation's capital and elsewhere are defying the Court's decisions upholding an individual right to bear arms as affirmed by the Supreme Court in Heller and McDonald. We support firearm reciprocity legislation to recognize the right of law-abiding Americans to carry firearms to protect themselves and their families in all 50 states. We support constitutional carry statutes and salute the states that have passed them. We oppose ill-conceived laws that would restrict magazine capacity or ban the sale of the most popular and common modern rifle. We also oppose any effort to deprive individuals of their right to keep and bear arms without due process of law.

We condemn frivolous lawsuits against gun manufacturers and the current Administration's illegal harassment of firearm dealers. We oppose federal licensing or registration of law-abiding gun owners, registration of ammunition, and restoration of the ill-fated Clinton gun ban. We call for a thorough investigation—by a new Republican administration—

of the deadly "Fast and Furious" operation perpetrated by Department of Justice officials who approved and allowed illegal sales of guns to known violent criminals.

The Fourth Amendment: Liberty and Privacy

Affirming the Fourth Amendment "right of the people to be secure in their houses, papers, and effects, against unreasonable searches and seizures," we call for strict limitations on the use of aerial surveillance on U.S. soil, with the exception of patrolling our national borders for illegal entry and activity. We oppose any attempts by government to require surveillance devices in our daily lives, including tracking devices in motor vehicles.

In recent years, technology companies have responded to market demand for products and services that protect the privacy of customers through increasingly sophisticated encryption technology. These increased privacy protections have become crucial to the digital economy. At the same time, however, such innovations have brought new dangers, especially from criminals and terrorists who seek to use encryption technology to harm us. No matter the medium, citizens must retain the right to communicate with one another free from unlawful government intrusion. It will not be easy to balance privacy rights with the government's legitimate need to access encrypted information. This issue is too important to be left to the courts. A Republican president and a Republican Congress must listen to the American people and forge a consensus solution.

The Foreign Account Tax Compliance Act (FATCA) and the Foreign Bank and Asset Reporting Requirements result in government's warrantless seizure of personal financial information without reasonable suspicion or probable cause. Americans overseas should enjoy the same rights as Americans residing in the United States, whose private financial information is not subject to disclosure to the government except as to interest earned. The requirement for all banks around the world to provide detailed information to the IRS about American account holders outside the United States has resulted in banks refusing service to them. Thus, FATCA not only allows "unreasonable search and seizures" but also threatens the ability of overseas Americans to lead normal lives. We call for its repeal and for a change to residency-based taxation for U.S. citizens overseas.

The Fifth Amendment: Protecting Human Life

The Constitution's guarantee that no one can "be deprived of life, liberty or property" deliberately echoes the Declaration of Independence's proclamation that "all" are "endowed by their Creator" with the inalienable right to life. Accordingly, we assert the sanctity of human life and affirm that the unborn child has a fundamental right to life which cannot be infringed. We support a human life amendment to the Constitution and legislation to make clear that the Fourteenth Amendment's protections apply to children before birth.

We oppose the use of public funds to perform or promote abortion or to fund organizations, like Planned Parenthood, so long as they provide or refer for elective abortions or sell fetal body parts rather than provide healthcare. We urge all states and Congress to make it a crime to acquire, transfer, or sell fetal tissues from elective abortions for research, and we call on Congress to enact a ban on any sale of fetal body parts. In the meantime, we call on Congress to ban the practice of misleading women on so-called fetal harvesting consent forms, a fact revealed by a 2015 investigation. We will not fund or subsidize healthcare that includes abortion coverage.

We support the appointment of judges who respect traditional family values and the sanctity of innocent human life. We oppose the non-consensual withholding or withdrawal of care or treatment, including food and water, from individuals with disabilities, newborns, the elderly, or the infirm, just as we oppose euthanasia and assisted suicide.

We affirm our moral obligation to assist, rather than penalize, women who face an unplanned pregnancy. In order to encourage women who face an unplanned pregnancy to choose life, we support legislation that requires financial responsibility for the child be equally borne by both the mother and father upon conception until the child reaches adulthood. Failure to require a father to be equally responsible for a child places an inequitable burden on the mother, creating a financial and social hardship on both mother and child. We celebrate the millions of Americans who open their hearts, homes, and churches to mothers in need and women fleeing abuse. We thank and encourage providers of counseling, medical services, and adoption assistance for empowering women experiencing an unintended pregnancy to choose life. We support funding for ultrasounds and adoption assistance. We salute the many states that now protect women and girls through laws requiring informed consent, parental consent, waiting periods, and clinic regulation. We condemn the Supreme Court's activist decision in Whole Woman's Health v. Hellerstedt striking down commonsense Texas laws providing for basic health and safety standards in abortion clinics.

We applaud the U.S. House of Representatives for leading the effort to add enforcement to the Born-Alive Infant Protection Act by passing the Born-Alive Abortion Survivors Protection Act, which imposes appropriate civil and criminal penalties on healthcare providers who fail to provide treatment and care to an infant who survives an abortion, including early induction delivery whether the death of the infant is intended. We strongly oppose infanticide. Over a dozen states have passed Pain-Capable Unborn Child Protection Acts prohibiting abortion after twenty weeks, the point at which current medical research shows that unborn babies can feel excruciating pain during abortions, and we call on Congress to enact the federal version. Not only is it good legislation, but it enjoys the support of a majority of the American people. We support state and federal efforts against the cruelest forms of abortion, especially dismemberment abortion procedures, in which unborn babies are literally torn apart limb from limb.

We call on Congress to ban sex-selection abortions and abortions based on disabilities — discrimination in its most lethal form. We oppose embryonic stem cell research. We oppose federal funding of embryonic stem cell research. We support adult stem cell research and urge the restoration of the national placental stem cell bank created by President George H.W. Bush but abolished by his Democrat successor, President Bill Clinton. We oppose federal funding for harvesting embryos and call for a ban on human cloning.

The Democratic Party is extreme on abortion. Democrats' almost limitless support for abortion, and their strident opposition to even the most basic restrictions on abortion, put them dramatically out of step with the American people. Because of their opposition to simple abortion clinic safety procedures, support for taxpayer-funded abortion, and rejection of pregnancy resource centers that provide abortion alternatives, the old Clinton mantra of "safe, legal, and rare" has been reduced to just "legal." We are proud to be the party that protects human life and offers real solutions for women.

The Ninth Amendment: The People's Retained Rights

The Ninth Amendment to the Constitution declares that "[t]he enumeration in the Constitution of certain rights shall not be construed to deny or disparage others retained by the people." This provision codifies the principle that our national government derives its power from the governed and that all powers not delegated to the government are retained by the people. We call upon legislators to give full force to this fundamental principle. We welcome to our ranks all citizens who are determined to reclaim the rights of the people that have been ignored or usurped by the federal and intrusive state governments.

Appendix C
Resolutions Passed by the
Republican National Committee

Pro-Life

2013

**RESOLUTION SUPPORTING RELIGIOUS FREEDOM
AND HOBBY LOBBY**

WHEREAS, A Health and Human Services regulation
promulgated to enable "The Affordable Care Act of 2010" also
known as "Obamacare" now demands that employers pay for
the contraceptive methods of their employees, including drugs
that cause abortion; and

WHEREAS, these abortifacients violate the first "unalienable
right," the right to life (written in the Declaration of

Independence) with which all human beings are endowed by their Creator and which is a preeminent tenet of Judeo-Christian religions; and

WHEREAS, Hobby Lobby, the craft store giant, operating over 500 stores in 42 states and employing over 13,000 full-time employees eligible for health care, will be forced to pay for insurance coverage that violates the religious principles held by owner, founder, and CEO David Green; and

WHEREAS, Hobby Lobby has provided health care for employees who are eligible; however, if the store refuses to comply with this new provision it could face a $1.3 million per day in government fines; and

WHEREAS, Hobby Lobby has filed suit stating that, under the First Amendment to the Constitution, which states that Congress shall not pass laws prohibiting the free exercise of religion, the federal government does not have the authority to force a business to participate in a program that violates the business owner's religious principles; and

WHEREAS, David Green, who has operated his company since 1970 according to his religious beliefs, has stated, "we seek to honor God by operating the company in a manner consistent with Biblical principles"; therefore, be it

RESOLVED, that the Republican National Committee stands with and commends the courageous actions of Mr. Green and Hobby Lobby to defend his right to operate his company according to his strongly and consistently held traditional religious principles.

As adopted by the Republican National Committee on January 25, 2013

RESOLUTION TO REDISTRIBUTE PLANNED PARENTHOOD FUNDING

WHEREAS, Planned Parenthood's most recent annual report stated that during fiscal year 2011- 2012, Planned Parenthood received a record $542 million in taxpayer funding in the form of government grants, contracts, and Medicaid reimbursements; and

WHEREAS, Taxpayer funding consists of 45% of Planned Parenthood's annual revenue; and WHEREAS in 2011, Planned Parenthood performed a record high 333,964 abortions; and

WHEREAS, over the past three reported years (2009-2011), Planned Parenthood has performed nearly one million abortions (995,687); and

WHEREAS, in 2011, abortions made up 92% of Planned Parenthood's pregnancy services, while prenatal care and adoption referrals accounted for only 7% (28,674) and 0.6% (2,300), respectively; and

WHEREAS, for every adoption referral, Planned Parenthood performed 145 abortions; and

WHEREAS, despite Planned Parenthood's claims that it offers women's healthcare services, cancer screening and prevention services provided by Planned Parenthood have dropped by 29% since 2009; and

WHEREAS, Planned Parenthood reported $87.4 million in excess revenue, and more than $1.2 billion in net assets; therefore, be it

RESOLVED, that the Republican National Committee calls upon Democrats and Republicans in Congress and the President to ensure that women do not suffer from lack of cancer screening and preventative services, by directing that such amounts as are currently being used by Planned Parenthood for screening will be diverted to organizations that specialize in cancer screening for women and who have not cut back on those services.

As adopted by the Republican National Committee on January 25, 2013

RESOLUTION SUPPORTING CORE VALUES OF THE 2012 REPUBLICAN PLATFORM

WHEREAS, the 2012 Republican Platform states, "our rights come from God, are protected by government, and that the only just government is one that truly governs with the consent of the governed," (Preamble, p. i); and

WHEREAS, the 2012 Republican Platform states, "Faithful to the "self-evident" truths enshrined in the Declaration of Independence, we assert the sanctity of human life and affirm that the unborn child has a fundamental individual right to life which cannot be infringed. We support a human life amendment to the Constitution and endorse legislation to make clear that the Fourteenth Amendment's protections apply to the unborn children" (We The People: A Restoration of the Constitution, p. 13-14); and

WHEREAS, the 2012 Republican Platform states, "We uphold the right of individuals to keep and bear arms, a right which antedated the Constitution and was solemnly confirmed by the Second Amendment" (We The People: A Restoration of Constitutional Government, p. 13); and

WHEREAS, the 2012 Republican Platform states, "We believe that marriage, the union of one man and one woman must be upheld as the national standard, a goal to stand for, encourage, and promote through laws governing marriage," and "We embrace the principle that all Americans should be treated with respect and dignity," (Renewing American Values to Build

Healthy Families, Great Schools and Safe Neighborhoods, p. 31); and

WHEREAS, the 2012 Republican Platform states, "The greatest asset of the American economy is the American worker," and "Just as immigrant labor helped build our country in the past, today's legal immigrants are making vital contributions in every aspect of our national life," and "Their industry and commitment to American values strengthens our economy, enriches our culture, and enables us to better understand and more effectively compete with the rest of the world"; and

WHEREAS, the 2012 Republican Platform further states, "Illegal immigration undermines those benefits and affects U.S. workers. In an age of terrorism, drug cartels, human trafficking, and criminal gangs, the presence of millions of unidentified persons in this country poses grave risks to the safety and the sovereignty of the United States," and "Our highest priority, therefore, is to secure the rule of law both at our borders and at ports of entry" (Reforming Government to Serve the People, p. 25); therefore be it

RESOLVED, the Republican National Committee reaffirms our commitment to the core values of the Republican Party as stated in the 2012 Republican Platform approved by the delegates to the Republican National Convention on August 28, 2012.

As adopted by the Republican National Committee on April 12, 2013

2014

RESOLUTION ON REPUBLICAN PRO-LIFE STRATEGY

WHEREAS, The Democrats have waged a deceptive "War on Women" attack against Republican pro-life candidates, demonizing them and manipulating American voters; and

WHEREAS, The Republican Party is proud to stand up for the rights of the unborn and believe all Americans have an unalienable right to life as stated in The Declaration of Independence; and

WHEREAS, Pro-life Republicans should fight back against deceptive rhetoric regardless of those in the Republican Party who encourage them to stay silent; and

WHEREAS, Candidates who stay silent on pro-life issues do not identify with key voters, fail to alert voters to the Democrats' extreme pro-abortion stances, and have lost their elections; and

WHEREAS, According to the extensive polling conducted by Gallup since 1975, many Republican stances regarding abortion garner at least 60 % support from the public and across the political spectrum:

- 87% support informed-consent laws about certain possible risks of the abortion
- 80% support banning abortion during the 3rd trimester;
- 71% support parental consent laws;
- 69% support imposing a 24-hour wait period before an abortion procedure;
- 64% of Americans support banning abortion during the 2nd trimester;
- 64% support banning partial-birth abortion;
- 64% support spousal notification laws that require the husband to be simply notified if his wife seeks an abortion; and

WHEREAS, Staying silent fails because this strategy allows Democrats to define the Republican brand and prevents the Republican Party from taking advantage of widely supported pro-life positions listed above to attract traditional and new values voters; and

WHEREAS, Staying silent fails to alert voters to the Democrats' extreme pro-abortion stances, which voters are repelled by; therefore be it

RESOLVED, The Republican National Committee condemns the Democrats' deceptive "war on women" rhetoric;

RESOLVED, The Republican National Committee will support Republican pro-life candidates who fight back against Democratic deceptive "war on women" rhetoric by pointing out the extreme positions on abortion held by Democratic opponents;

RESOLVED, The Republican National Committee will not support the strategy of Republican pro-life candidates staying silent in the face of such deceptive rhetoric; and,

RESOLVED, The Republican National Committee urges all Republican pro-life candidates, consultants, and other national Republican Political Action Committees to reject a strategy of silence on the abortion issue when candidates are attacked with "war on women" rhetoric.

As adopted by the Republican National Committee on January 24, 2014

RESOLUTION ON PAIN-CAPABLE UNBORN CHILD PROTECTION LAWS

WHEREAS, Republicans have championed the sanctity of human life in our National Party Platform for nearly four decades; and

WHEREAS, the Democratic Party has become the party of pro-abortion extremism, dropping even the wish that abortion be "rare" from their party's platform; and

WHEREAS, led by the state of Nebraska in April 2010, 14 states have now enacted versions of Pain-Capable Unborn

Child Protection laws, almost always by overwhelming margins, recognizing the reality of pain in the unborn and providing legal protection for the unborn at 20 weeks (almost 5 months) of pregnancy and beyond; and

WHEREAS, on June 18, 2013, the U.S. House of Representatives voted to pass the national Pain-Capable Unborn Child Protection Act to provide legal protection for the unborn at 20 weeks of pregnancy and beyond in the United States; and

WHEREAS, as of March 18, 2014, at least 40 Republican members of the U.S. Senate have co-sponsored the companion bill to the House-passed legislation; however, the Democrats in control continue to callously approve of this barbaric practice; and

WHEREAS, substantial medical evidence confirms that the unborn child is capable of experiencing pain at least by 20 weeks, if not earlier; and

WHEREAS, public opinion polls on abortion after almost 5 months of pregnancy show that Americans believe this practice should be banned; 80 percent of Americans oppose abortion in the third trimester and 64 percent reject abortion after 12 weeks while 63 percent of women believe it should not be permitted after the point where substantial medical evidence says the unborn child can feel pain; and

WHEREAS, late-term abortion is emotionally and physically harmful to women, destructive of the ethical norms and reputation of the medical profession, and offensive to the canons of law, medicine, and society that require us to protect the weak from the strong, the powerless from the powerful; therefore be it

RESOLVED, the Republican National Committee reaffirms its core principle of the sanctity of human life in our party platform for nearly four decades, namely, that the unborn child has a fundamental individual right to life that cannot be infringed; and be it further

RESOLVED, that the Republican National Committee strongly supports federal, state, and local pain-capable unborn child legislation that bans abortions at 20 weeks (almost 5 months) of pregnancy and beyond.

As adopted by the Republican National Committee
on May 9, 2014

2015

RESOLUTION TO DEFUND PLANNED PARENTHOOD AND PREVENT THE USE OF ILLEGALLY OR UNETHICALLY OBTAINED FETAL TISSUE IN RESEARCH

WHEREAS, In the 1984 *National Organ Transplant Act,* Congress criminalized the buying and selling of organs for profit so that organizations would not profit by the sale of human organs for transplant, intentionally making the sale of human organs illegal in the United States; and

WHEREAS, Senior medical officers of Planned Parenthood were seen in recent videos negotiating prices for fetal organs and tissue in violation of these laws that prevent the sale of human tissue, and human organs and tissues can come only from human beings; and

123

WHEREAS, The human beings killed by abortion cannot give consent for the donation of their organs, so it is not possible to ethically obtain fetal tissue through an elective abortion; and

WHEREAS, Senior medical officers of Planned Parenthood discussed how they would alter the abortion procedure to retrieve these fetal organs and tissue in violation of the law that requires an abortion to be performed in such a way as to ensure the mother's safety only; and

WHEREAS, Planned Parenthood receives more than $500 million in taxpayer money every year; therefore be it

RESOLVED, That the Republican National Committee requests that Congress pass the *No Taxpayer Funding for Abortion and Abortion Insurance Full Disclosure Act (S. 582)* to enact a permanent, government-wide prohibition of taxpayer funding for abortion to ensure that taxpayer money is never used for the killing of innocent life or the sale of body parts of aborted babies;

RESOLVED, That the Republican National Committee calls on all branches of the United States government, including the

National Institutes of Health, and State Governments to cease funding the use in research of these illegally and/or unethically obtained human organs and tissues obtained through elective abortions;

RESOLVED, That the Republican National Committee urges relevant law enforcement agencies to prosecute the employees of Planned Parenthood who profited personally or for their organizations from the sale of human organs; and

RESOLVED, That the Republican National Committee insists that Congress specifically defund Planned Parenthood immediately to make it clear that such unlawful behavior in violation of human dignity cannot be condoned.

As adopted by the Republican National Committee on August 10, 2015

About Phyllis Schlafly

Phyllis Schlafly was a national leader of the
conservative movement since the publication of her best-
selling 1964 book, *A Choice Not An Echo* which was updated
and re-issued in 2014. She was a leader of the pro-family
movement since 1972, when she started her national volunteer
organization called Eagle Forum. The *Ladies' Home Journal*
named her one of the 100 most important women of the 20th
century.

Mrs. Schlafly is the author or editor of 27 books and
served as a member of the Commission on the Bicentennial of
the U.S. Constitution, 1985-1991, appointed by President
Reagan. She has testified before more than 50 Congressional
and State Legislative committees on constitutional, national
defense, and family issues.

Phyllis Schlafly is America's best-known advocate of the dignity and honor that we as a society owe to the role of full-time homemaker. The mother of six children, she was the 1992 Illinois Mother of the Year. She passed away on September 5, 2016.

About Ed Martin

On September 28, 2015, Phyllis Schlafly named Ed Martin as her hand-picked successor. Ed had been working as a special assistant to Phyllis for more than two years. A lawyer and bioethicist by training, Ed had previously served as chairman of the Missouri Republican Party and chief of staff to Missouri Governor Matt Blunt. Ed lives in St. Louis, Missouri, with his wife and four children.